D1320899

A Young Citizen's Guide To:

Local
Government

Richard Tames

W

HODDER
Wayland

A Young Citizen's Guide series

Parliament
Local Government
The Electoral System
Central Government
The Criminal Justice System
Voluntary Groups
The Media in Politics
The European Union
Money
Political Parties

Published in Great Britain in 2001 by Hodder Wayland, a division of Hodder Children's Books

Editor: Patience Coster
Series editor: Alex Woolf
Series design: Simon Borrough
Picture research: Liz Gogerly/Glass Onion Pictures
Consultant: Dr Stephen Coleman

British Library Cataloguing in Publication Data
Tames, Richard, 1946-
A young citizen's guide to local government
1. Local government - Great Britain - Juvenile literature
2. Great Britain - Politics and government - 1997-
Juvenile literature
I. Title
320.8'0941

ISBN 0 7502 3775 9

Printed in Hong Kong by Wing King Tong Co. Ltd.

Hodder Children's Books, a division of Hodder Headline Limited, 338 Euston Road, London NW1 3BH

Picture acknowledgements: the publisher would like to thank the following for permission to reproduce their pictures: Mary Evans Picture Library 8, 11; Photofusion 13 (David Tothill), 21 (Liam Bailey), 26 (Peter Olive), 27 (Paul Doyle), 28 (Peter Olive), 29 (Liam Bailey); Popperfoto/Reuters 15, 25; Press Association/Topham 4, 16, 17, 23; Scotland in Focus 19 (R G Elliott); Topham/ImageWorks 14; Topham Picturepoint 5, 7 (top), 7 (bottom), 10, 12, 18, 22, 24; Wayland Picture Library 9, 20.

Cover:
City chambers, Glasgow (R Weir/Scotland in Focus); street sweeper (Topham Picturepoint); trading standards officer (David Tothill/Photofusion); policewoman and firefighter (Wayland Picture Library).

Contents

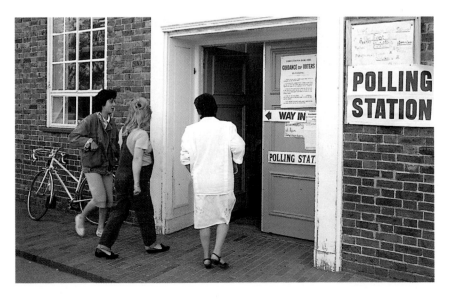

What Is Local Government?

Local government organizes services, such as street cleaning, for a community as a whole.

Local government runs the services and facilities we need in everyday life. These include schools, housing, roads, parks, libraries, leisure centres, street cleaning, refuse collection and home helps. Local government has powers which can make a real difference to people's lives by improving their environment and their chances of employment. If local government runs smoothly, you hardly know it exists: it's like electricity – you only notice it when it fails.

Local government is divided into councils, authorities and boroughs. It employs over two million people and spends a quarter of all the money collected in taxes. The rest of the money collected in taxes is spent by central government, which is responsible for services the whole country needs such as defence, the health service, universities, prisons, the legal system and Britain's relations with other countries. The central government, which is based in Westminster, London, allocates most of the money spent by local government, sets out its major duties and checks that they are carried out.

Parish politics There is also a lower layer of local government consisting of 10,000 parish or community councils. These control minor matters, such as footpaths and signposts, public clocks and memorials, parks, open spaces and play areas, litter bins, allotments and bus shelters. Some parish councils own a village hall. They may support local charities, clubs and community organizations by helping them to get funding, for instance.

Parish councils usually have a representative on the board of governors of their local primary school. Parish councils put forward local views about planning applications for new buildings or roads, or alterations to them or changes in their use. They do not have the power to approve or reject planning applications – this is done at a higher level. Not all parishes have a parish council. North Yorkshire, for example, has 700 parishes but only 437 councils.

Parish councils pay attention to the details of community life, such as organizing signing for public rights of way.

How is local government organized?

Five different types of local authority run local government in England:

1. **34 county councils**
2. **238 district councils (the county councils are divided into these)**
3. **36 metropolitan councils**
4. **46 unitary authorities**
5. **32 London boroughs**

County councils mostly have the same boundaries as the historic 'shires' into which England was subdivided for a thousand years. Metropolitan councils are usually based on old-established cities. Unitary authorities often have a mixture of urban and rural communities. The London boroughs exclude the ancient City of London, which is still governed by its own Lord Mayor who serves for one year and chairs the City's ruling bodies.

Scotland and Wales consist entirely of unitary councils – 32 and 22 respectively – though some bear the names of traditional counties (Pembrokeshire, Denbighshire), parts of counties (South Ayrshire) or cities (Aberdeen, Dundee). The six counties of Northern Ireland are also split into 26 separate councils.

Why do we need local government?

1. Locally elected councils can draw on councillors' knowledge of their community to take account of public feeling or special local conditions.

2. Local government has some power to collect local taxes and spend the money as it wishes. It can therefore experiment with new ways to help the community.

3. Local government allows people to take part in democratic decision-making on matters that affect their everyday lives. Britain's 26,000 local councillors include higher proportions of women, ethnic minorities and manual workers than Parliament does.

4. Local government informs and influences central government on matters such as local crime, transport and education, helping to ensure that central government takes notice of the world outside Westminster between elections.

5. Decisions at local level can be made faster and often better than if they had to be sent in to central government.

6. Local councils co-ordinate activities that affect each other closely, such as planning, housing and roads or education, libraries and skills training.

7. Local government can attract new businesses or visitors to the community and so create more or better jobs.

8. Local government can make the community safer. Some councils have passed by-laws to ban drinking alcohol in public places. Others have installed CCTV systems to cut crime.

9. Local government can help to train politicians to go further in public life. One quarter of all Conservative Members of Parliament and almost half of all Labour MPs have served as local councillors.

10. Local government can improve the environment by encouraging the recycling of waste and by controlling nuisances and pollution.

Direct democracy?

Traditionally, local government decisions are made by councillors who have been elected by local voters. The referendum (a direct vote on a single issue) offers an alternative way of making at least some decisions. In 1999, Brighton council held an advisory referendum about 'Bringing the Blues Home'. Over the years the local football team, Brighton and Hove Albion, had slipped down the divisions, had money problems and was forced to sell its ground. In the referendum, Brighton council asked whether it should go ahead with a scheme to build a new home stadium for the Albion. On one hand, the project was likely to create many jobs; on the other, it involved building in an area of outstanding natural beauty. Over 67,000 people turned out to vote (more than had turned out in the local election), many of whom had never bothered to vote about anything before. This encouraged the council to go ahead – with special safeguards against traffic and litter nuisances. The referendum cost £30,000 – enough to employ a local primary school teacher for a year. Do you think this was money well spent? What would you hold a referendum about in your area?

Mobile libraries, bottle banks (above) and free bus passes for pensioners all began as local experiments which were then copied by other local governments.

John Major, Prime Minister between 1990 and 1997, was once a local councillor in South London.

From Magistrates to Managers

Five hundred years ago, Britain was a country of villages and small towns. Local government in the countryside relied on the unpaid hard work of landowners who were sworn on oath to serve the king as magistrates, known as Justices of the Peace (JPs). To be chosen to serve as a JP was a mark of honour and could lead to higher office or the reward of a knighthood. The work took up many hours and was very varied. JPs had to see that criminals were arrested, that roads and bridges were kept in good repair and beggars were moved on. They also had to check that the wages and prices paid and the weights and measures used by tradesmen were as the law required.

Being a nightwatchman was an unpopular duty – many were elderly and ill-equipped to catch criminals.

Towns were governed by a mayor and council, chosen by leading tradesmen from among their own ranks. Mayors were chosen from the senior, longest-serving councillors, known as aldermen. The actual work of arresting criminals, supervising the market-place and seeing that refuse was cleared up was done by house owners serving in rotation, rather than by paid officials. Because many people could not read or write, a professional clerk was often paid to keep records of taxes, court decisions, letters and so on. Most men could expect to serve a term as constable or nightwatchman at least a couple of times in their lives.

Victorian changes

Up until the nineteenth century the tasks of local government were carried out by amateurs. Then the rapid growth of industry and huge cities created problems that the old system could not cope with. Public health was the most urgent. Many towns had grown so rapidly that they had no proper drains or water supply and much slum housing. The conditions were ideal breeding-grounds for disease.

The idea that the better-off people in a community had the right to invite each other to take turns in running local affairs was challenged. Critics said that traditional town councils were often incompetent, lazy and corrupt. As more people learned to read, newspapers became increasingly critical of mayors and councils who failed to control pollution and epidemics.

From the 1830s onwards, town councils were reformed so that they were elected by house owners who paid a local tax known as a rate. Revenue raised from rates was used to pay for local services. Qualified, full-time professionals were appointed to serve as Medical Officer of Health, Borough Surveyor and Borough Engineer, to tackle urgent environmental problems by providing paved streets, drains, water supplies, public bath-houses and cemeteries and improving waste disposal. As a result of their efforts, death rates fell dramatically.

In medieval times, Justices of the Peace enforced fair trading in shops and markets.

'Local government units formed a jungle.... Haverfordwest in Pembrokeshire enjoyed the same privileges as the City of London.... By 1750 Halifax parish had 50,000 inhabitants yet still no acting JP... reforms ... to improve street lighting or policing... sprang from local initiatives.... The result was a crazy patchwork.... There was no national rhyme or reason in the siting of new... roads... such things were never decided nationally.... '
Professor Roy Porter, *English Society in the Eighteenth Century.*

As the environmental problems were overcome, attention shifted to providing new facilities and services to make life better, such as street lighting, parks and libraries. In the countryside the work of JPs was gradually cut back to dealing with minor crimes and licensing public houses. In 1888 local government in rural areas was turned over to elected county councils.

Town halls run the towns

By the first half of the twentieth century, Britain had become overwhelmingly a nation of town-dwellers for whom borough councils provided a wide range of services and facilities. These included:

- education – running schools, technical colleges and libraries;
- housing and environment – building houses and flats to rent, controlling the standards of private builders, cleaning streets and collecting refuse;
- transport – maintaining roads and bridges and running bus and tram services;
- health and welfare – running hospitals, mental homes, clinics, public bath-houses and homes for senior citizens;
- utilities – providing clean water supplies and often gas, electricity and even telephone services too;
- business – building and supervising markets;
- leisure – running theatres and sports facilities.

The architecture of Birmingham town hall recalled the dignity of the city-states of ancient Greece.

INFERIOR BATH.

ENTRANCE TO THE ST. PANCRAS BATHS AND WASHHOUSES.

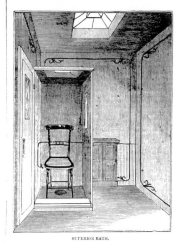
SUPERIOR BATH.

Victorian reformers believed that cleanliness was 'close to godliness'. Providing facilities for 'the great unwashed' to bathe became a national movement.

Providing these many services meant that in large cities like Liverpool 'the Corporation' was often the biggest local employer. Its efficiency could make a great difference to a community's prosperity.

From running services to regulating them

Since the 1980s, the idea that local government should itself provide a wide range of services has changed dramatically. Instead, local authorities are now encouraged to employ private businesses (contractors) to provide services such as buses, street cleaning and the maintenance of roads and buildings. The idea is that firms competing with each other for contracts to do such work will offer better value than an authority's own employees, who know that they have the job whether or not they perform well. A contractor who performs badly can simply be replaced. According to this view, the main task of local government is now to set standards for providers of public services and to see that they are achieved. This marks a big shift from actually providing services to regulating the providers instead. What matters now is 'best value'.

'In an unrepresentative and inefficient system corruption and jobbery of all kinds were rampant. Officials often used and manipulated municipal property to their advantage. Large salaries, banquets, and bribes absorbed tax money.'
Goldwin Smith, in *A Constitutional and Legal History of England*, describing the situation in local government prior to the reforms instituted by the Municipal Corporations Act of 1835.

Local government supervises a range of facilities and services. In the UK more than 8,000,000 pupils are taught in some 25,000 schools by more than 300,000 full- or part-time teachers. Almost a billion pounds is spent on 15,000 libraries, which employ a staff of more than 22,000. As libraries have become computerized and able to provide internet access, they offer a means of spreading skills and information that can benefit local businesses.

Local authorities also maintain parks, leisure centres and sports facilities, such as swimming pools, golf courses and tennis courts. Some authorities support local theatres. They are also responsible for conserving aspects of local heritage through museums, galleries and the upkeep of monuments. Heritage services benefit not only education but tourism as well.

Environmental services Although far
fewer people live in council-owned homes than was once the case, the number still amounts to millions. Local authorities are responsible for administering housing benefit. They work closely with semi-independent housing associations to up-grade existing

Some local authorities have closed down playgrounds in case an accident leads to a legal claim for compensation. Do you think children's safety should be the responsibility of parents or of local government?

homes or to build new ones, especially in inner city areas. And they remain responsible for planning permissions involving privately built housing, shops or businesses. Other local authority tasks include road maintenance, street lighting, refuse collection, street cleaning, removing abandoned vehicles and recycling waste, together with environmental protection measures, ranging from food safety to air pollution. Councils employ over 100,000 social workers and care staff to provide personal social services such as domestic help, to run old people's homes and to look after children with special needs.

Consumer protection

Local authorities employ trading standards officers to prevent the sale of fake, unsafe or defective products. They check up on 'use by' dates on perishable goods and on scales, weights and measuring instruments used in shops. They inspect storage facilities for petrol, poisons and explosives to make sure that they are safe. They also look at accusations of unfair trading from people buying goods and services in the local area. Trading standards officers work closely with the Citizens' Advice Bureau and usually have a telephone helpline to deal quickly with complaints and enquiries. Citizens' Advice Bureaux are funded by local government but staffed mainly by volunteers who are well-informed about consumer and family matters.

Trading standards officers are the front-line force for detecting faulty or fake goods and prosecuting offenders.

'All development – from the big housing estate or shopping centre to the individual house extension or conversion and the location and size of advertisements – must obtain... planning permission from the local council. Where such permission is refused, appeal may be made to the Minister.... There are some 650,000 such appeals a year in England and 40,000 in Scotland... the Minister rarely overturns the decision of the local authority.'
Tony Byrne, *Local Government in Britain.*

Have you got a licence for that?

Local authorities are responsible for issuing licences to control a wide range of trades and activities, including taxis, employment agencies, childminders, nursing homes, cinemas, theatres, stables, kennels, street-collecting for charities, dealing in game, gun-ownership and waste disposal. In most cases this involves inspecting premises or ensuring that regulations are being followed. Local authorities also employ over 20,000 firefighters, and are responsible for planning arrangements to meet major emergencies such as flooding, chemical pollution or bomb scares.

Checks and balances There are

many checks and balances built into the system to ensure that local government does its job properly. Local councillors oversee the work of council officers and employees. While one political party may control a council, it can be sure that its decisions will be questioned by councillors of other parties or by independents. Journalists working for local newspapers, radio or television are always on the lookout for a story. Organized groups in the community, such as residents' and tenants' associations, the local chamber of commerce (representing local businesses), trades councils (on behalf of local trade unions), neighbourhood watch schemes, conservation groups, arts groups, ethnic groups and parents' associations are all likely to contact local councillors. They will attend council meetings or even demonstrate in protest if they feel their interests are being neglected or over-ridden.

The Audit Commission checks that local government money has been spent legally and efficiently. OFSTED inspects the work of teachers in schools, and the

Youth services are provided by a partnership between local government and voluntary organizations, involving half-a-million volunteers.

Social Services Inspectorate monitors social and care workers. Finally, a person dissatisfied with their treatment by a local council can complain to the local government Ombudsman, who may require the council to justify its action and force it to remedy a fault if it is found to have behaved unfairly or below standard.

Firefighters help a householder to safety during a period of flooding.

Check it out!
Councils use 'performance indicators' to check how well they are providing services. Each year the results of these are published to show how they are improving. Here are some examples of performance indicators:
- **percentage of phone calls answered within five rings**
- **number of complaints referred to the local government Ombudsman**
- **number of racial incidents recorded**
- **number of council-owned buildings with disabled access**
- **number of council publications available in large print or Braille, or on audiotape or in ethnic minority languages**
- **number of tons of rubbish recycled**
- **percentage of street lights working properly**
- **amount spent per pupil in schools**
- **standard of test and examination results in schools**
- **number of books, videos etc. loaned by libraries**
- **percentage of users satisfied with council services**

How is your local council doing? You can find out by checking the details on your council's internet web site.

A hundred years ago most of the money spent by local authorities was raised by them from their own communities, either from rates (taxes on local properties, such as houses and businesses) or from charges made for the services they provided. This meant that local authorities had a good deal of freedom to decide how to spend their money. Now a far higher proportion of local authority income is received in the form of grants from central government. This means that local authorities have less control over setting their own priorities.

Where the money comes from

The main sources of local government income are:

- grants from central government (about 50 per cent);
- local taxes – council tax (about 12 per cent), which is paid by local residents (with exemptions e.g. for students); and business rate (about 18 per cent), which is paid by local businesses;
- fees (including rents) and charges (about 18 per cent) e.g. for use of leisure centres, car parking;
- borrowing, mainly to finance major projects such as building a new library or swimming pool.

Other sources of money include the European Union, the National Lottery and special funds from central government for particular schemes, such as reviving inner-city areas. Councils can also raise money by selling off buildings or land that they own.

> 'Too often within a council the members and officers... decide what services are to be provided on the basis of what suits the council.... The interests of the public come a poor second best... more spending and more taxes are seen as the simple solution rather than exploring how to get more out of the available resources.'
>
> From *Modern Local Government in Touch with the People*, published by the Department of the Environment, Transport and the Regions, 1998.

Schools represent the biggest single item of local government spending.

What it is spent on According to local government financial statistics of 1998, spending by UK local government as a whole can be divided into current (about £70 billion a year) and capital (about £7 billion). Current means day-to-day spending on wages, supplies (fuel, printing) and paying off loans. Capital means spending on items of long-term value like roads or buildings.

Education is the biggest single item of local government current spending, and accounts for a third of the total. Housing, social services (home helps, old people's homes) and emergency services (fire and police) each account for between 13 per cent and 16 per cent, environmental services (cleaning, refuse collection) 7 per cent and transport 5 per cent. Housing is the largest item under capital spending, accounting for about 40 per cent, followed by transport (18 per cent), environmental services (17 per cent) and cultural services – the arts, libraries, education, museums (14 per cent).

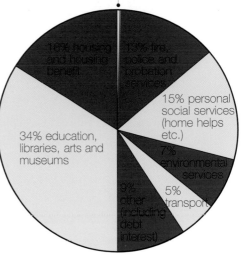

1% sport and recreation

16% housing and housing benefit

13% fire, police and probation services

15% personal social services (home helps etc.)

34% education, libraries, arts and museums

7% environmental services

9% other (including debt interest)

5% transport

A chart showing local government gross expenditure by category. Central government sets upper levels for local government spending and borrowing.

After major emergencies or disasters, local authorities may qualify for cash help from central government to pay off extra costs or repair damage.

Contracts and corruption

Because local authorities handle huge sums of money and are responsible for awarding major contracts for building, catering, maintenance and supplies of materials, the possibility of corruption exists. For this reason, strict standards of auditing (checking the books) are enforced to ensure that money is properly spent and that the best value for money is achieved. The Audit Commission is the organization that carries out most of this work, but some councils have officials whose full-time job is to check against fraud. Councillors or local government officers convicted of accepting bribes or 'favours' (such as free holidays) can expect heavy fines and/or prison sentences.

Promoting prosperity

During the first half of the twentieth century, seaside towns traditionally co-operated with railway companies to share the costs of advertising their attractions through posters and newspapers. In this way they increased the number of visitors, which was profitable both for the resort and the railway that took them there. Now almost every local authority has an employee whose responsibility it is to attract visitors, if not as tourists then to attend conferences or exhibitions.

In the past, local authorities advertised to attract visitors – now they encourage investors as well.

Local authorities also try to attract businesses to set up in their areas. To this end, they co-operate with Training and Enterprise councils to improve the pool of skilled labour available locally.

The Dis-United Kingdom?

Patterns of local government differ throughout England, Wales, Scotland, Northern Ireland and the offshore islands of the British Isles. The Isle of Man, the Channel Islands, the Isles of Scilly, the Orkneys, Shetland Islands and Western Isles (Outer Hebrides) each have their own separate arrangements for local government.

Far out – Stornoway town hall in the Western Isles. Will less central government control mean greater local power?

All change The organization of local government has changed repeatedly over the last thirty years. For example, in 1974 the new counties of Avon, Cleveland and Humberside were created, but these were abolished in 1996. In the same year many new unitary authorities were created. Some ancient counties, like Suffolk, Norfolk, Hertfordshire and Cornwall, remained unchanged. But several others had densely populated areas that did not correspond to major cities. These became the new unitary authorities of Bracknell Forest, the Medway towns, Torbay and Thurrock.

Who cares? The many changes that have taken place in the organization of local government mean that people are often confused about which bodies are responsible for providing what services. This may be one reason for the generally low level of public interest in local government. Only three people out of every hundred claim to be 'very interested' in local affairs. Nine out of ten people cannot name their local councillor. The turnout at local elections is falling. In the 1980s it averaged around 40 per cent, today it averages around 30 per cent, under half that of general elections for Parliament. In some areas, turnouts as low as 10 per cent have been recorded. These United Kingdom figures are in striking contrast with other European countries, such as Italy, Belgium and Denmark, where the turnout at local elections is more than 80 per cent.

Schools, community centres and village halls usually serve as polling stations during local elections.

The low voter turnout in UK local elections may also be caused by the following factors:

- people move home much more frequently now than they once did, so they are less involved in a community than if they had lived there for many years;
- many people live in an area controlled by one local authority but spend most of their waking hours working elsewhere in a different one;
- some areas, especially in London, have thousands of foreign residents living there for only short periods of time – these people are not entitled to vote; other cities have large student populations who are much more involved in their college than in the surrounding community.

We care! Just because people are not very interested in local government does not mean that they want to do away with it. Opinion surveys repeatedly show that:

- a large majority would prefer the level of local taxes to be decided by local councils rather than by central government, as is usually the case;

- the majority of people want *less* central control of local government rather than *more* central control;
- more than twice as many people are satisfied with the performance of local government than are satisfied with the performance of central government;
- two-thirds of the public think they get good value for money from local government; over a five-year period, just under one in ten people will make contact with an MP, but one in five will make contact with a local councillor.

Getting involved in student politics can be a first step towards getting involved in local politics.

Quangos Communities are also affected by the decisions and work of other official bodies that are not part of local government as such. Most of these are 'quangos' (quasi-autonomous non-government organizations) which spend almost as much tax money as local government does. Quangos are run by people appointed by central government, rather than elected by local voters. Examples include:

- NHS trusts which run hospitals;
- police authorities, which control police forces;
- Training and Enterprise councils (soon to be replaced by Learning and Skills councils), which exist to improve the skills of workers;
- regional development agencies, which aim to improve investment, employment and development in the nine regions into which England is divided.

'We can see the power the Scottish Parliament gives them at the bargaining table. We've had a fairly consistent demand... for the development of a regional government with powers at least as strong as those of the Welsh Assembly.'
Ian Mearns, councillor for Gateshead in Tyne & Wear. Recently there has been increased demand for more powers for regional government in some parts of England. Support appears to be especially strong in the North-East. In Prime Minister Tony Blair's constituency, Sedgefield, a survey showed 72 per cent in favour of a vote to create a regional assembly.

London – a special case

London has its own separate structure of government. This reflects the fact that it is not only the nation's capital but also by far the largest city, with about one in eight of the country's entire population. It is also the hub of Britain's national and international communications. Local government in London is broken down into the following structures.

- the City of London – the self-governing 'Square Mile' which still elects its own Lord Mayor each year and has its own police force. More than 400,000 people work in the City but only about 4,000 actually live and vote there.
- London boroughs – thirty-two in all, including Westminster, which is called a City. These are the main providers of local services such as schools, housing, libraries and so on. They range from some of the richest areas in Britain (Kensington & Chelsea) to some of the very poorest (Hackney, Newham, Tower Hamlets).
- In 2000 London gained a directly elected mayor and assembly. Together they make up the Greater London Authority which is responsible for decisions that affect London – especially transport, planning, police and fire services, the environment, health, the arts and tourism.

'Since *all* on a local council are responsible... *none* is clearly accountable.... The public cannot clearly apportion blame and credit.... Local government is a headless state... responsibility... needs to be dramatized, clarified and exposed instead of obscured... by the committee system. Such highlighting... would be best achieved by focusing it upon one person.'
Professor D Regan, University of Nottingham.

More a country than a city? London's population equals those of Scotland and Wales added together.

Mayors – back to the future?

The City of London chooses a new Lord Mayor every year. On the second Saturday in November, the newly elected Lord Mayor rides in a colourful procession to the Royal Courts of Justice to swear his loyalty to the Queen. Along the route, money is collected from the crowds for a charity chosen by the new Lord Mayor, whose main task is to be a sort of ambassador, promoting London as a world centre of finance. The Lord Mayor's year in office is filled with speeches, meetings, banquets and entertaining important foreign guests.

The lord mayors or mayors of other major cities take part in their government but also spend much of their time on ceremonial duties. Manchester's Lord Mayor, for example, is involved in opening new public facilities, giving out awards and fund-raising for good causes through events such as carol concerts or fun runs. The main business of running Manchester as a city is headed by a Chief Executive Officer, who is appointed rather than elected.

Candidates for the mayoralty of London. Winner Ken Livingstone is fourth from the right.

In 2000, Ken Livingstone became the first mayor in London's history to be directly elected by its voters. (The Lord Mayor of the 'Square Mile' of the City of London still continues to serve as before.) Livingstone has pledged to tackle London's transport problems as his top priority. Many people believe his four-year term of office is a major experiment in city management. If he succeeds in making London work better, and if he gets more Londoners interested in its government, the post of directly elected mayor may be copied in other major cities.

New duties, less power During the 1980s and 1990s, local government finances came increasingly under central government control. Local authorities lost control of many aspects of education and housing; and services such as refuse collection, buses and buildings maintenance were handed over to private contractors. But local authorities gained new responsibilities in areas such as environmental protection and publishing information about council activities.

Town twinning Town twinning aims to build links between communities in different countries in the interest of international friendship and understanding. Britain's first twinning relationship, dating from 1920, was between Keighley, Yorkshire and Poix du Nord, France. There are now over 1,900 twinned communities in the UK. Most have links with the USA or countries in the European Union, but there are also links with Asian, Latin-American and Commonwealth countries. Links with eastern European countries are growing fast. Since 1989 town twinning has been organized by the Local Government International Bureau. In the past, twinning usually involved social, cultural and educational exchanges through visits by choirs, sports teams, language students and clubs of gardeners, dancers, farmers or other special interest groups. Recently, exchanges have broadened to take in working groups, such as firefighters or health specialists. Twinned communities have also begun to share their experiences of tackling environmental problems or helped each other to attract investors and tourists.

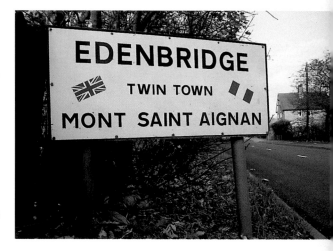

Twinning of individual towns may lead on to twinning of regions to co-operate across national boundaries.

The ceremonial head of the council may be called the Chairman, Mayor or Lord Mayor and represents the council on public occasions such as the opening of a new public building. The leader of the council (usually the leader of the political party with the largest number of elected councillors) is in charge of political matters. Major decisions, budgets and appointments are decided at full council meetings, which all elected councillors attend.

Getting elected

To be elected as a councillor, a person must be over the age of twenty-one and registered to vote within the local authority upon whose council they wish to serve. They must have lived or been employed there for at least one year and be a citizen of the UK, Ireland or a Commonwealth country. They also need the written support of at least ten local voters. Local authority employees are not allowed to stand as councillors of the authority they work for, but may stand as councillors in other authorities. No one who has been found guilty of corruption or illegally interfering with elections or has served more than three months in prison in the previous five years is eligible to stand. To vote in a local election a person must be over eighteen years of age, a local resident and a citizen of the UK or European Union. Councillors serve for four years before facing re-election.

The traditional robes worn by a Lord Mayor date from three centuries ago and include an official chain of office with the city's coat of arms.

Most of the election candidates are chosen to represent a particular political party. Some candidates stand on behalf of community groups or as independents; this is especially the case in country areas, where party politics tends to be less important than in towns.

I protest! In any five-year period, about one person in twenty takes part in a protest march. But far more people than this use their vote in a local election. In this way they can show their displeasure with the government in Westminster by voting for candidates of the opposite political party. Control of councils can therefore switch from one party to its rival, even though the existing council may have been doing a perfectly reasonable job.

Like MPs, local councillors need to meet voters in large numbers face to face at election times.

What councillors do Councillors are community leaders who help to define how a community needs to tackle its problems, such as street crime, and to achieve its goals, such as healthier lifestyles. Councillors oversee public services and make sure that the local authority treats local people fairly and efficiently. Councillors are local representatives of the ward that elected them. In a five-year period, about one in five voters is likely to contact their local councillor with an enquiry or complaint about housing, schools or social services. Most councillors hold regular 'surgeries' where voters can meet them face to face.

A matter of trust
In December 1988 the local government Ombudsman found Westminster City Council officials at fault for failing to stand up to local councillors when they disagreed about selling off local cemeteries: 'Members (councillors) believed... that some officers were intent on 'sabotaging' their policy of running the council on more business-like lines. Officers felt that their service to the council... was not valued and that members did not trust them.... But officers have a duty to give advice to all members even when they suspect it will be unpalatable. Here they failed in their duty.'

If councillors do not have the power to deal with a matter they can often advise a person about who can help them best. Councillors are not paid a salary but receive an attendance allowance and expenses. Those willing to work long hours can receive the equivalent of an average wage.

Committees, committees Although the full council approves all major decisions, in practice most of these are made in detail by councillors working in committees. These deal with particular tasks such as finance, housing, education and highways etc. Large committees often have smaller sub-committees to speed up routine decision-making or to prepare reports or recommendations on particularly difficult issues. On average, councillors spend about one hundred hours a month in committee meetings. Committees recommend decisions to meetings of the full council. If they are routine matters, the council usually approves them without further discussion. If the decision is controversial or has major, long-term effects, there is likely to be a full debate and a formal vote.

Full meetings of a local authority council take place with members of the press and public looking on.

Officials In the past, council officers were appointed for their professional expertise. The town clerk was often a trained lawyer, the finance officer an accountant, the borough surveyor an architect or engineer. Today more emphasis is placed on broader skills, such as the ability to build up effective teams of employees, to develop information systems, or to manage change and monitor the performance of individuals and departments in setting and achieving targets.

Local Government for the Twenty-First Century

Further changes are on the way for local government. Major aims include getting more people interested and taking part in local affairs; making local government more efficient and better value for money; and increasing the availability of information about and access to services.

The central government in Westminster wants to see local councillors spending less time in committees and more time keeping in touch with the people they represent and visiting the businesses, charities and organizations in their community. It also wants to end the traditional system by which the same councillors make decisions and check up on how they are being carried out. The aim is to reach decisions more quickly, with more openness, and to ensure that these decisions are more carefully checked up on.

Market research methods can be used to keeping constant touch with public concerns and attitudes.

Techniques and technology

Companies marketing new products use questionnaires and 'focus groups' to find out what customers want. Political parties have increasingly used such market research methods to help them win elections. Local government is being encouraged to follow this lead. England's oldest recorded city, Colchester in Essex, has established a citizens' panel of 1,250 people, chosen to provide a cross-section of local opinion on what the council's main priorities should be.

New technologies, like the internet and email, make it possible for people to find out more about local affairs and to provide local authorities and councillors with almost instant feedback.

> 'Local decision-making should be less constrained by central government and also more accountable to local people.'
> Labour Party election manifesto, 1997.

New local government, new Britain

Local government must continue to change, because Britain is changing. Older people are living longer, therefore more services must be geared to their needs. As more people retire early and remain fit for longer, there are greater opportunities for volunteers to take part in community affairs.

The number of single-parent and single-person households is increasing. This means that more childcare services need to be set up, so that single parents can work. It also means that fewer 'family size' homes are required. As the European Union introduces more consumer protection regulations, the task of enforcing them will fall to local trading standards officers. Other European Union rules will affect environmental controls, health and safety and employment conditions. To combat global warming, local authorities will be required to improve energy efficiency in such matters as housing, waste disposal and transport. Meeting international challenges will depend on effective local, as well as national, action.

Activity
Write to your local council, or consult its web site and look at the performance indicators from the past year. Then divide your class into pairs and have each pair decide which you think are the most important indicators (e.g. rubbish collection, transport etc.) Allocate a points system based on your conclusions, and then report to the others how well you think the council has performed.

As more parents work outside the home, there is an increasing need for childcare facilities.

Glossary

absorbed used up

administer to run a system or activity

allotment a patch of ground used for growing vegetables or flowers

amateur not professionally trained

borough a town or part of a city with legal powers of self-government

bribe money or gift taken in return for a favour

CCTV closed-circuit television

constable an official appointed to enforce the orders of a magistrate

contract a legal agreement

co-ordinate to organize things to work smoothly together

corruption taking money or favours to use official powers illegally or unfairly

defective not working properly

incompetent unable to do a job properly

jobbery making a private profit out of holding a public position

magistrate a judge with powers to try minor cases but not trained as a professional lawyer

metropolis a very large city

neighbourhood watch a voluntary organization of local inhabitants supported by the police; its function is to report suspicious characters and hooligans.

nightwatchman a local official paid to patrol a town by night to guard against criminals. Many nightwatchmen were ex-servicemen, honest and loyal but sometimes too old or disabled to tackle thugs.

Ombudsman an official appointed to examine complaints

parish a local community centred around a church

performance indicator an item or action that can be counted or measured to show how well something is done

planning permission the legal go-ahead needed before permanent building work can begin

premises a building or place used for work

rampant out of control

recycling collecting and converting waste materials for re-use

representative a person chosen to speak or act on behalf of a group of people

revenue income

rotation in turn

slum a run down or overcrowded building

unitary authority local government units which replaced the old two-tier system of county and district councils

ward a district into which a city, town or parish is divided for administration and election of representatives etc.

Resources

Almost every major local authority has its own web site, giving details of its organization, services and publications, and the names of councillors and senior officials. The minutes of council meetings are usually available in the main branches of public libraries. Many libraries now have free online access to local authority web sites.

The following national web sites are also useful sources of information:

http://www.local-regions.detr. gov.uk/
The Department of Environment, Transport and the Regions – UK DETR – the main department of central government with responsibility for the finances and performance of local government

http://www.lgiu.gov.uk
The Local Government Information Unit

http://www.gwydir.demon.co.uk/ uklocalgov/
UK local government information

http://www.gwydir.demon.co.uk/ uklocalgov/localgov.htm
UK local government – England and Wales

http://www.slgiu.gov.uk
Scottish Local Government Information Network

http://www.psr.keele.ac.uk/local htm
Local and regional government web pages

http://www.nalc.gov.uk
National Association of Local Councils, provides up-to-date information on changes in local government

http://www.lgce.gov.uk
Local Government Commission for England – advises on organizational issues, such as changes in boundaries

http://www.open.gov.uk/lgof
Local Government Ombudsman – deals with complaints about local government

http://www.lgao.org.uk
Local Government Audit Office – checks local government finances and performance indicators

http://www.info4local.gov.uk
Information for local government

http://www.pamis.gov.uk/
Parliamentary Monitoring and Intelligence Service – provides information for local government about what central government is doing that might affect its work

http://www.lgib.gov.uk/
Local Government International Bureau – deals with links with local authorities overseas, such as town-twinning

http://www.clip.gov.uk
Central and Local Government Information Partnership – deals with links between central and local government

http://www.idea.gov.uk
Improvement and Development Agency

http://www.nlgu.org.uk
New Local Government Network – organizations promoting change and improvement in local government

http://www.lgn.co.uk
Local Government News

http://www.lgc.net.com
Local Government Chronicle – newspapers covering local government matters

http://www.tradingstandards. gov.uk/
Trading Standards Council – deals with consumer rights

Visit www.learn.co.uk for more resources.

Index